DEC 1 7 2008

COOL HELPING CAREERS

METEOROLOGIST

By Geoffrey M. Horn

Reading Consultant: Susan Nations, M.Ed.,
author/literacy coach/consultant in literacy development

Gareth Stevens
Publishing

Please visit our web site at **www.garethstevens.com.**
For a free catalog describing Gareth Stevens Publishing's list of high-quality books, call 1-800-542-2595 (USA) or 1-800-387-3178 (Canada).
Gareth Stevens Publishing's fax: 1-877-542-2596

Library of Congress Cataloging-in-Publication Data
Horn, Geoffrey M.
   Meteorologist / by Geoffrey M. Horn.
      p. cm.—(Cool careers)
   Includes bibliographical references and index.
   ISBN-10: 0-8368-9194-5   ISBN-13: 978-0-8368-9194-2 (lib. bdg.)
   ISBN-10: 0-8368-9327-1   ISBN-13: 978-0-8368- 9327-4 (softcover)
   1. Meteorology—Vocational guidance—Juvenile literature.   2. Meteorologists—Juvenile literature.   I. Title.
   QC869.5.H67   2008
   551.5092—dc22   2008005653

This edition first published in 2009 by
Gareth Stevens Publishing
A Weekly Reader® Company
1 Reader's Digest Rd.
Pleasantville, NY 10570-7000 USA

Senior Managing Editor: Lisa M. Herrington
Editor: Joann Jovinelly
Creative Director: Lisa Donovan
Designer: Paula Jo Smith
Photo Researcher: Kimberly Babbitt

Picture credits: Cover, title page: Joe Raedle/Getty; pp. 4–5 Jim Watson/AFP/Getty Images; p. 6 © Graham Neden/Ecoscene/Corbis; p. 7 Brian Bahr/Getty Images; pp. 8–9 © Visuals Unlimited/Corbis; p. 11 Ida Mae Astute/ABC/Courtesy Everett Collection; pp. 12–13 © Visuals Unlimited/Corbis; p. 13 © Justin Lane/epa/Corbis; p. 14 AP Images; p. 15 Reuters/Corbis; p. 16 AP Images; p. 17 © Jim Edds/Corbis; p. 18 © Jim Reed/Corbis; p. 19 © 2008 AccuWeather.com; pp. 20–21 AP Images; p. 22 map: Weekly Reader; pp. 22–23 © Chuck Doswell/Visuals Unlimited/Corbis; p. 24 Shutterstock; p. 26 © Hans Strand/Corbis; p. 27 global warming diagram: Weekly Reader; p. 28 © Jim Reed/Corbis

Printed in the United States of America

1 2 3 4 5 6 7 8 9 10 09 08

CONTENTS

Words in the glossary appear in **bold** type the first time they are used in the text.

CHAPTER 1
SEEING DANGER, SAVING LIVES

L ife turned upside-down for the people of Greensburg, Kansas, on May 4, 2007. The emergency warning came at 9:25 P.M. That's when sirens sounded. Everyone who heard the sirens knew what they meant. A tornado was coming. People had to find shelter — *immediately*.

The safest place to be when a twister strikes is below ground in a basement, away from windows. People in Greensburg who didn't have a basement went to neighbors who did. Others found shelter in basements of the courthouse or schools. When people came out of their shelters later that night, most of their town was gone.

Sounding the Warning

The twister that hit Greensburg had winds of more than 200 miles (320 kilometers) per hour. Eleven people were killed. At least sixty more were injured.

A tornado wrecked Greensburg, Kansas, but early warnings helped most people escape the savage storm.

Houses blew apart. Churches and shops were ruined. Although the toll was terrible, it could have been much worse. Many lives were saved because of one person — Mike Umscheid.

Umscheid is a **meteorologist** — a scientist who studies the weather. He was on duty the night the tornado hit. At first he thought the twister would bypass Greensburg. When he saw the monster storm turn toward the town, he issued the emergency.

Weather Stations

Weather stations are found throughout the world. They help meteorologists predict and track weather. The stations have different instruments to measure weather. For example, an **anemometer** is a device that measures wind speed. A thermometer measures **temperature**.

A weather station at Halley Bay, Antarctica

What Is Meteorology?

Thousands of people like Mike Umscheid have jobs in **meteorology**. Meteorology is the study of Earth's **weather** and **atmosphere**. The word comes from two ancient Greek words. *Meteoros* means "high in the air." *Logos* means "reason."

Meteorologists are sometimes called atmospheric scientists. They study clouds, wind, and rain patterns. They try to understand how Earth gets warmer or cooler. They look for better ways to predict the weather.

How Meteorologists Help

Meteorologists have an important job. If they do their work well, many lives may be saved. Meteorologists alert people when hurricanes and floods threaten their homes. They warn farmers when **drought** endangers their crops. They also caution pilots when wind, ice, or snow makes it dangerous for planes to take off or land.

What will the weather be like tomorrow? Will it be too snowy for school? Is it too chilly for a picnic? Will rain cancel the baseball game? Meteorologists let us know what to expect.

When meteorologists predict a long, heavy rain, baseball teams roll out the tarp to keep the infield from getting soaked.

CHAPTER 2

FORECASTING THE WEATHER

Meteorologists do different jobs. Some work for television stations and other media to **forecast**, or predict, the weather. Many work for the National Weather Service (NWS). The NWS is the main government weather agency. The military uses meteorologists. So do private companies. These companies provide forecasts to farmers and others who depend on the weather. Some meteorologists do advanced work in science. They study changes in Earth's **climate**.

A meteorologist studies different weather maps before coming up with a forecast.

Television and Radio Forecasters

You've probably heard forecasters talk about the weather on TV or radio. These forecasters study weather data and present it on air. They tell you what you need to know right away. Will a hurricane slam into your town?   If so, your family may need to board up its windows. Will it rain tonight?   Better pack that umbrella. Will temperatures drop from mild

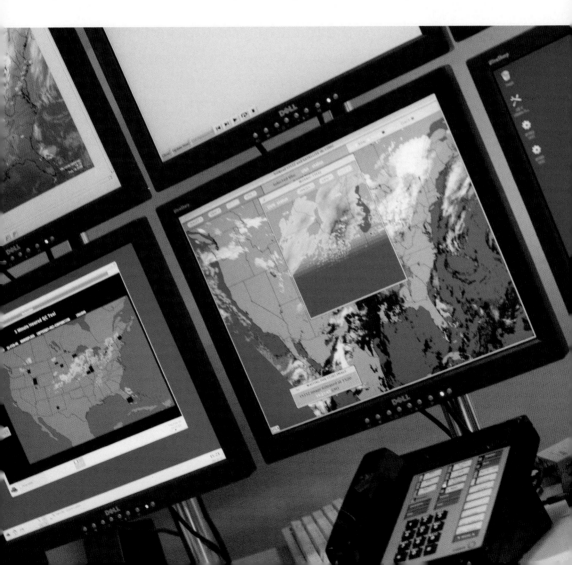

to chilly? Time to cover up that short-sleeved shirt with a jacket. TV and radio jobs are hard to get, but they often pay well. Some forecasters have become famous on local and national TV.

Government Forecasters

Not all weather forecasters work in front of the camera. Some meteorologists forecast weather for the government or the military. Many work for the NWS, which provides local weather forecasts to TV and radio stations that don't have meteorologists, in addition to serving the government. The NWS keeps track of weather patterns from more than a hundred years ago. This government agency also provides warnings about severe weather such as hurricanes and tornadoes.

Climate Scientists

Weather forecasters focus on weather for the short-term. But climate scientists spend their days researching long-term weather patterns. They study the world's climate. They try to predict weather trends in the years to come.

Climate scientists divide the world into climate zones. Zones can be hot or cold. They can also be wet or dry. For example, the Sahara Desert in North Africa has a dry climate. The Amazon rain forest in South America is different. Its tropical climate is warm and wet. Sometimes climate zones can be a mix of conditions.

On the Job: TV Forecaster

Sam Champion broadcasts the weather for ABC's *Good Morning America*. To try to figure out what the weather will bring, Champion studies data and makes his forecast. "People like to think that forecasts are exact, and they're not," he said. "The weather is *always*, *always* changing."

Meteorologists rely on computers and other high-tech tools.

Today, many climate scientists are focused on **global warming** — Earth's rise in temperature. They are working to find out how rising temperatures will affect Earth's future.

How to Become a Meteorologist

For jobs in meteorology, people need college degrees in climate science or a related field. To prepare for a career in this field, students should take high school and college classes in Earth science, chemistry, physics, math, and computer science. For advanced research, many years of study may be needed.

Is Meteorology Right for Me?

Are you curious about the world? Do you get excited when a storm approaches? Most meteorologists were students who enjoyed science. They became curious about the changes that create weather. Are you interested in working with computers and other research tools? Do you want to help people? If so, then a career in meteorology might be right for you.

On the Job: Climate Scientist

James Hansen works for the U.S. government. He has become an expert on climate. He was one of the first scientists to warn about global warming. Today, Hansen continues his climate research. "We have to focus on energy efficiency and renewable sources of energy," he says.

CHAPTER 3

TOOLS OF THE TRADE

How did people predict the weather in the past? They looked for signs in nature. For example, people in England once thought that if they saw a pig chewing straw, rain was on the way. They also believed that a full moon could chase away the clouds. Today, meteorologists use scientific tools to forecast the weather.

A weather satellite took this photo of Hurricane Ivan in 2004 as It headed toward the Caribbean island of Jamaica.

Radiosonde

Many tools to measure weather have been invented. One very powerful device dates from the 1920s. This device is the **radiosonde**. The radiosonde is a small, lightweight box. Inside it are tools that measure temperature, **humidity**, and air pressure. It also has a small radio transmitter.

Groundhog Day

People today still believe **superstitions** that predict the weather. The most famous example takes place on February 2 each year. People in Punxsutawney, Pennsylvania, gather to watch a groundhog named Phil come out of his burrow. If he sees his shadow, people claim that winter will last six more weeks.

radiosonde

A weather researcher releases a weather balloon, with a radiosonde attached.

A weather balloon carries the radiosonde high into the air. As it rises, it sends out radio signals. These signals report on weather conditions. Weather scientists launch balloons around the world each day. Students sometimes help to prepare these balloons. They supply meteorologists with important data.

Aircraft

The invention of airplanes gave meteorologists another tool to track weather. Airplanes let people fly into severe weather, such as hurricanes. The planes have equipment to record weather data. These missions can be very dangerous. But they give meteorologists the most up-to-date information on big storms.

Hurricane Hunters

Meteorologists who love excitement can join a team of hurricane hunters. These groups fly directly into hurricanes! A flight crew and a meteorologist must work together quickly. The crew releases a small device called a **dropsonde**. Once inside the hurricane, it records wind speed, temperature, and humidity. This information is transmitted back to the airplane, where the meteorologist reviews it. Weather forecasters use the data to predict the path and strength of a hurricane.

Braving ferocious winds, hurricane hunter Raymond Tong tracked Hurricane Ophelia in 2005.

dropsonde

Radar

Another important tool is **radar**. Radar uses pulses of energy to look deep inside clouds. A special tool called Doppler radar can show how fast clouds are moving. It can also show which clouds will make the most **precipitation**. Forecasters can then predict how much rain will fall in an area. If necessary, they can issue flood warnings. Doppler radar is also helpful for telling meteorologists the direction in which a tornado is moving.

Weather Satellites

Weather satellites circle the globe. They measure temperature, wind speed, and other weather changes

A severe storm shows up in yellow and red on Doppler radar.

Highs and Lows

The air is like a blanket that surrounds Earth. Meteorologists measure the weight of air pressing down on Earth. This measurement is called air pressure. If you look at a weather map, you may see areas marked "H" or "L." The "H" marks an area of high pressure. The "L" marks an area of low pressure. High pressure areas usually bring warm, dry weather. Low pressure areas tend to bring cooler, wetter weather.

from high above Earth. They help meteorologists track hurricanes and other big storms. Satellites provide forecasters with information about weather over oceans and other far-off areas.

Computers

Until the 1950s, weather maps were drawn by hand. Today, meteorologists use high-speed computers. These computers can analyze very complex data. They can produce maps showing the weather right now — or days, weeks, or years from now. Such tools help meteorologists make more accurate forecasts.

CHAPTER 4
WILD WEATHER

Bad weather can strike anywhere, at any time. In August 2005, Hurricane Katrina slammed into the Gulf Coast. It was one of the worst disasters in American history. More than 1,800 people in Louisiana and Mississippi were killed. Hurricanes are just one type of wild weather that meteorologists track every day.

Mighty Hurricanes

Hurricane season in the United States lasts from June through November. Hurricanes start as **tropical storms** over warm ocean waters. They form when warm, moist air rises from the ocean's

After Hurricane Katrina hit New Orleans, rescue workers used boats to save residents of the flooded city.

surface. Violent winds and thick clouds swirl around a calm center called the eye. Inside the clouds are strong thunderstorms with heavy rain. Meteorologists start tracking tropical storms early, before they grow into dangerous hurricanes.

Hurricanes can cause damage in several ways. Strong winds blow roofs off houses and rip trees from

Slow Comeback

Meteorologists worked around the clock before Hurricane Katrina hit land. They warned that the city of New Orleans, Louisiana, was in terrible danger. Today, New Orleans still struggles to recover. Before the storm hit, the city had about 450,000 residents. By the end of 2007, only about 300,000 people were living in the city.

the ground. Hurricane winds also blow water from the ocean onto the land. This type of flood is called a storm surge. Farther inland, heavy rains may also cause flooding.

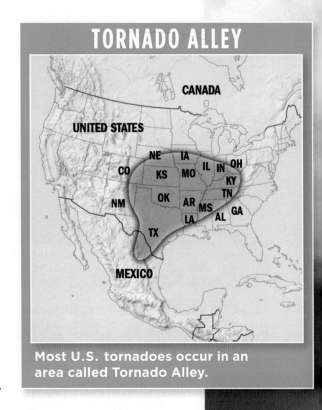

TORNADO ALLEY

Most U.S. tornadoes occur in an area called Tornado Alley.

A tropical storm becomes a hurricane when winds reach at least 74 miles (119 km) an hour. But some hurricanes are stronger. Just before Hurricane Katrina hit the United States, it packed winds of up to 175 miles (282 km) per hour.

Terrifying Tornadoes

Tornadoes can strike in any month in any part of the world. In the United States, most tornadoes strike between April and July. Many twisters form in an area that includes Oklahoma and nearby states. This area is called **Tornado Alley**. Here, hot air traveling north from the Gulf of Mexico collides with cool, dry air from Canada. This creates large thunderstorm clouds. Sometimes the rising air begins to spin, forming a

When a funnel cloud touches the ground, a tornado unleashes its full fury.

funnel-shaped cloud. When the funnel-shaped cloud touches ground, it turns into a tornado.

When conditions are right for tornadoes, meteorologists warn the public. They also contact government officials so they can keep people safe. A few meteorologists work as tornado chasers. They drive toward tornadoes and take pictures from their cars. This job can be very risky — even for people with a lot of experience.

Lightning is powerful,
beautiful, unpredictable
— and deadly.

When Lightning Strikes

Meteorologists say that at any one time about
1,800 storms around the world are creating lightning.
Lightning is a giant electric spark that starts in a rain
cloud. Most lightning goes from cloud to cloud. Some
travels from a cloud to the ground.

The air near a lightning bolt can get up to five times
hotter than the surface of the Sun! The intense heat
from lightning causes the surrounding air to expand.
This makes a loud sound called thunder. Thunder is
nature's warning to go inside. Meteorologists warn:
"When thunder roars, go indoors."

Lightning strikes the ground in the United States about 25 million times each year! Although getting hit by lightning is unlikely, meteorologists alert people when a storm is coming so they stay safe.

Blinding Blizzards

Most of the time, snow means winter fun — sledding, skiing, or a day off from school. But a heavy snow or ice storm can be very dangerous. A blizzard is a winter storm that combines heavy snow with winds of at least 35 miles (56 km) per hour. In a blizzard, drivers may be unable to see the cars in front of them. Meteorologists send out warnings ahead of time so people can stay off the roads.

El Niño and La Niña

Meteorologists look for clues when forecasting the weather. One important clue is El Niño (NEEN-yoh). In normal years, the Pacific Ocean is warmer in the west than in the east. In an El Niño year, however, the waters of the eastern Pacific also become warm. This affects weather throughout the world. In the United States, for example, the South gets more rain than usual.

El Niño occurs every two to seven years. La Niña often follows it. In a year of La Niña (NEEN-yah), waters in the eastern Pacific get cooler than usual. La Niña years tend to produce more hurricanes. Both El Niño and La Niña last for twelve to eighteen months.

CHAPTER 5

THE CHALLENGE OF CLIMATE CHANGE

If global warming continues to shrink polar ice caps, polar bears may not survive.

Meteorologists face challenges every day. They know that people depend on weather forecasts. Farmers want to know when it's safe to plant crops. Army leaders need to know when it's safe to move troops. People need to know when a big storm is coming.

Today, climate scientists face a new challenge. They need to understand global warming — the rise in Earth's temperature. They want to know exactly how and why our climate is changing.

SUN

Incoming heat from the Sun

Heat escapes into space

Heat is reflected back to Earth

Earth

Mixture of gases around Earth

Hot Stuff: Global Warming

Climate scientists say global warming is caused by pollution. Burning fossil fuels like oil and coal pollutes the air. When these fuels are burned, they send gases into the atmosphere. These gases trap heat from the Sun. They make our world warmer.

Warning Signs

Earth has warmed and cooled many times over its long history. But this time seems different. Temperatures are going up more quickly than before. Polar ice caps are melting. Sea levels are rising. Storms are getting wilder. Meteorologists will be needed to understand and deal with these challenges.

Meeting the Challenge

How much warmer will the world get? Scientists aren't sure. But even a change of a few degrees

Weather Record Breakers

Highest land temperature ever recorded:
Temperature: 136° F (57.8° C)
Place: El Azizia, Libya, in Africa
Date: September 13, 1922

Lowest land temperature ever recorded:
Temperature: -129° F (-89.4° C)
Place: Vostok, Antarctica
Date: July 21, 1983

Source: U.S. National Climatic Data Center

could change the environment. Some islands and coastal areas would vanish beneath the sea. Storms even more powerful than Hurricane Katrina could batter our shores. New diseases might spread. Plants and animals that need colder weather would die out.

What will our world look like in fifty or one hundred years? Can we keep the planet from getting warmer? Right now, meteorologists are helping to find answers to these important questions.

These storm chasers are meteorology students in south-central Kansas.

METEOROLOGIST

OUTLOOK

- The United States had about 8,800 meteorologists in 2006. That number will rise to about 9,700 by 2016.
- Many climate scientists work for the National Weather Service. Others work for the military or in colleges and universities. Private companies also hire climate experts.

WHAT YOU'LL DO

- Meteorologists hold many types of jobs.
- Some work alone, running small weather stations. Others work with teams of scientists to study weather data.
- A small number hold risky jobs as hurricane hunters or tornado chasers.
- You've probably seen weather forecasters on television. These TV jobs are scarce. But they often pay very well.

WHAT YOU'LL NEED

- For a job as a meteorologist, you'll need a college degree in climate science or a related field.
- To do research, you may need an advanced degree.
- To work as a storm chaser, you may need to know how to fly a plane.
- To report the weather on radio or TV, you'll need good speech and reporting skills.

WHAT YOU'LL EARN

- Meteorologists usually make between $55,000 and $96,000 a year. The starting salary may be as low as $36,000. About 10 percent of meteorologists earn $120,000 or more.

Source: U.S. Department of Labor, Bureau of Labor Statistics

GLOSSARY

anemometer — a scientific instrument used to measure wind speed

atmosphere — the blanket of air that surrounds Earth

climate — weather conditions measured over a long period of time

dropsonde — a small container attached to a parachute that includes devices for measuring the temperature, wind speed, and humidity inside a hurricane

drought — a long period of dry weather that causes water shortages and threatens crops

forecast — to predict something; also, the prediction itself

global warming — the rise in world temperatures believed to be caused when heat-trapping gases pollute the air

humidity — a measure of how much moisture the air contains

meteorologist — someone who studies Earth's atmosphere in order to forecast the weather and understand climate change

meteorology — the study of what happens in the atmosphere; also known as climate science or atmospheric science

precipitation — water that falls from the sky as rain, snow, sleet, or hail

radar — a system developed in the 1940s that uses radio waves to detect the location of moving and fixed objects

radiosonde — a small, lightweight box that includes devices for measuring the weather and a radio to transmit the data to a station on the ground

superstitions — false beliefs or practices

temperature — a measure of how hot or cold something is

Tornado Alley — an area of the United States where many tornadoes form

tropical storms — large storms that form over warm ocean waters

weather — conditions in the atmosphere at a particular place and time

TO FIND OUT MORE

Books

Earth's Weather and Climate. Planet Earth (series). Jim Pipe (Gareth Stevens, 2008)

Extreme Weather: Science Tackles Global Warming and Climate Change. National Geographic Investigates (series). Kathleen Simpson (National Geographic Children's Books, 2008)

Hurricane & Tornado. Eyewitness Books (series). Jack Challoner (DK Publishing, 2000)

Meteorologists. Scientist at Work (series). Heather Hammonds (Smart Apple Media, 2004)

Meteorology Projects With a Weather Station You Can Build. Build-a-Lab Science Experiments (series). Robert Gardner (Enslow, 2008)

Web Sites

EPA Climate Change Kids
epa.gov/climatechange/kids
> Learn the facts behind global climate change and what you can do about it.

National Weather Service
www.nws.noaa.gov
> Check out the official U.S. government web site for weather information.

The Weather Channel Kids
www.theweatherchannelkids.com
> Find out about careers in meteorology, play weather games, watch weather videos, and explore topics in the Weather Encyclopedia.

Publisher's note to educators and parents: Our editors have carefully reviewed these web sites to ensure that they are suitable for children. Many web sites change frequently, however, and we cannot guarantee that a site's future contents will continue to meet our high standards of quality and educational value. Be advised that children should be closely supervised whenever they access the Internet.

INDEX

About the Author

Geoffrey M. Horn has written more than three dozen books for young people and adults, along with hundreds of articles for encyclopedias and other works. He lives in southwestern Virginia, in the foothills of the Blue Ridge Mountains, with his wife, their collie, and six cats. He dedicates this book to the people of Greensburg, Kansas.